A BEGINNING BOOK OF

HOW SHIPS PLAY CARDS

BY CYNTHIA BASIL

PICTURES BY JANET MCCAFFERY

WILLIAM MORROW & COMPANY

NEW YORK 1980

Library of Congress Cataloging in Publication Data

Basil, Cynthia.
    How ships play cards.

    Summary: Uses riddles to introduce words that look and sound alike
but have different meanings.
    1. English language—Homonyms—Juvenile literature. [1. English
language—Homonyms] I. McCaffery, Janet. II. Title.
PE1595.B36   428   79-18420
ISBN 0-688-22217-X
ISBN 0-688-32217-4 lib. bdg.

When can a ribbon shoot arrows?

When it has a **bow**.

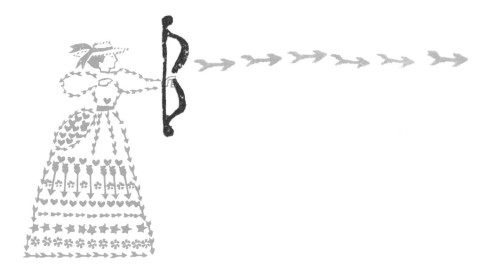

Bow may mean
a way to tie a ribbon,
a weapon that shoots arrows,
even a rainbow.

They are different things,
but they are also alike;
they all bend in a curve.
That's why they have the same name.

Words like *bow* are called "homonyms."
Hom- means "same," and *-onym* means "name."
Can you answer more riddles with them?

What paper is good to eat?

What road can eat dinner?

Paper in a **roll**.

A road with a **fork**.

Paper can be turned over and over,
or rolled, to make a roll.
And so can bread,
which makes a roll you eat.

The fork you eat with
is divided into parts called "tines."
A road has a fork
when it divides into new roads.

What's good on a roll but bad on a road?

Jam.
Lots of strawberries pressed, or jammed, together make a good fruit jam to eat on a roll.

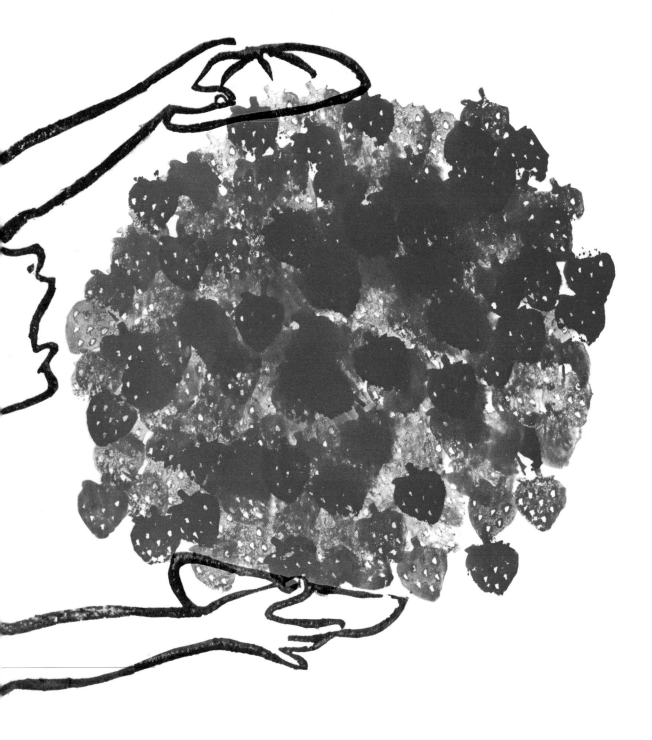

Lots of cars jammed together
make a bad traffic jam on a road.

When lots of boats sail together,
a river may have a traffic jam too.

What do some rivers have that all years have?

Falls.
When a river falls over a cliff,
it becomes a waterfall.

During the fall of every year
leaves fall from trees.

Why are trees and factories alike?

They are **plants**.
Trees and most other living plants
cannot move from place to place.
They are planted, or fixed, in one place.

And so are the factories,
or plants,
where people work.

What tree do you always have in your hand?

A **palm**.
Nobody knows exactly why
the inside of your hand is called a "palm."
But the palm tree got its name
because its leaves look like fingers
stretched out from a hand.

What fish is always part of your foot?

A **sole**.
The sole, or bottom, of your foot
was named after the *solea*,
a Roman shoe made of a flat piece of leather.
Some fish that live on the bottom of the sea
are called "sole" because they are flat too.

What part of you is a musical instrument?

An **organ**.

Organ comes from a word that means "work."
Your brain, heart, and lungs are a few of the organs
that work to keep you alive.

The organ that is a musical instrument
works when it makes music.

A piano makes music too.
But how does it unlock a door?

With one of its **keys**.
When you press the keys of a piano,
the parts inside move.

When you turn a key in a lock,
the parts inside it move.

A key can unlock the door to your house.
But how can tulips and daffodils light its rooms?

With their **bulbs**.

Tulips, daffodils, and some other plants
grow from bulbs.
The light bulb got its name
because many of them are shaped like plant bulbs.

Often with one word, like *bulb*,
you can name two things
that are different but also alike.

Can you name a bird
and shout, "Heads down!"
with one word?

Duck.
A duck dives and dips, or ducks,
head down into the water for food.

When you shout, "Duck!"
people duck their heads down too.

Change one letter in duck
to find out how ships play cards.

With a **deck**.
In a deck of playing cards
each card covers another.
A ship's deck covers part of the ship.

Many ships cross the ocean.
When a ship reaches land,
how does the ocean say good-bye?

With a **wave**.
The ocean moves up and down in waves.

Your hand and mine move up and down
when we wave good-bye.

About the Author

Cynthia Basil received a B.F.A. from Carnegie Institute of Technology (now Carnegie-Mellon University) and went on to graduate work in art history at the University of Chicago and New York University's Institute of Fine Arts.

After five years as a designer in a Washington, D.C., art studio, Ms. Basil moved to New York, where she now works as an art director. An inveterate collector, she has filled her home in Brooklyn Heights with the many unusual books and toys she has acquired.

About the Illustrator

Since her graduation from the Philadelphia College of Art, Janet McCaffery has illustrated over thirty books for children. In addition, she is active in the fields of advertising illustration and package design.

Even with the demands imposed by a busy career, Ms. McCaffery has found time to continue studies in drawing and painting at the School of Visual Arts. At present she makes her home in New York City.